This Is the Way We Build

Fabiola Sepulveda

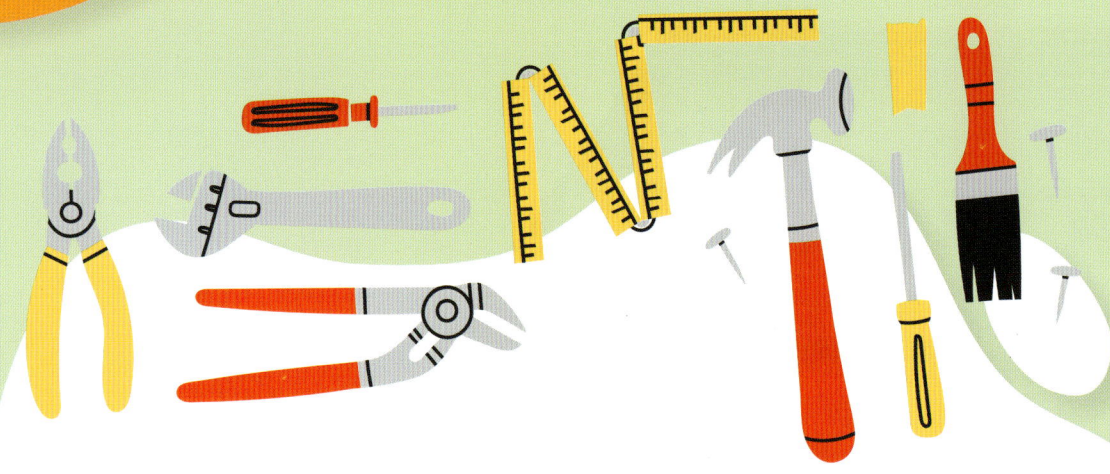

Notes for the Grown-ups

This wordless book allows for a rich shared reading experience for children who do not yet know how to read words or who are beginning to learn. Children can look at the pages to gather information from what they see, and they can suggest text to tell the story.

To extend this reading experience, do one or more of the following:

Before reading, talk about the materials and tools you might use to build. Then, read the book to see if any of those things are pictured.

Draw a building plan. Then, using cardboard, glue, scissors, crayons, and so on, construct small buildings.

Go for a walk to look at buildings in your area. Talk together about how they were made.

Introduce vocabulary such as these words when looking at the pictures and telling the story you see:

- architect
- brick
- building
- cement
- door
- hammer
- ladder
- nails
- paint
- scaffolding
- screws
- tiles
- window
- wood
- wrench

After reading the pictures, come back to the book again and again. Rereading is an excellent tool for building literacy skills.

Consultant

Cynthia Malo, M.A.Ed.

Publishing Credits

Rachelle Cracchiolo, M.S.Ed., *Publisher*
Emily R. Smith, M.A.Ed., *SVP of Content Development*
Véronique Bos, *VP of Creative*
Dona Herweck Rice, *Senior Content Manager*

Image Credits: all images from iStock and/or Shutterstock

Library of Congress Cataloging in Publication Control Number:
2024013721

TCM | Teacher Created Materials

5482 Argosy Avenue
Huntington Beach, CA 92649
www.tcmpub.com
ISBN 979-8-7659-6139-1
© 2025 Teacher Created Materials, Inc.
Printed by: 926. Printed In: Malaysia. PO#: PO11723